Add to your Maths skills with CGP!

This fantastic CGP book is exactly what pupils need to become champions of Year 2 Addition and Subtraction.

It's crammed full of quick-fire tests — each one takes 10 minutes. They get tougher throughout the book, building up the skills to take on adding and subtracting questions of all difficulties.

To top it off, we've included full answers to every question — plus a handy chart to check progress too!

What CGP is all about

Our sole aim here at CGP is to produce the highest quality books — carefully written, immaculately presented and dangerously close to being funny.

Then we work our socks off to get them out to you — at the cheapest possible prices.

Published by CGP

Editors: Sean McParland, Charlotte Sheridan and Ben Train

With thanks to Joanne Haslett and Caley Simpson for the proofreading.

With thanks to Jan Greenway for the copyright research.

ISBN: 978 1 78908 634 8

Graphics used throughout the book © www.edu-clips.com
Printed by Elanders Ltd, Newcastle upon Tyne.

Based on the classic CGP style created by Richard Parsons.

Text, design, layout and original illustrations © Coordination Group Publications Ltd. (CGP) 2020
All rights reserved.

Photocopying this book is not permitted, even if you have a CLA licence.
Extra copies are available from CGP with next day delivery • 0800 1712 712 • www.cgpbooks.co.uk

Contents

Test 1 2

Test 2 4

Test 3 6

Test 4 8

Test 5 10

Test 6 12

Test 7 14

Test 8 16

Test 9 18

Test 10 20

Test 11 22

Test 12 24

Answers 26

Progress Chart 30

How to Use this Book

- This book contains <u>12 tests</u>, all geared towards improving your addition and subtraction skills.

- Each test is out of <u>8 marks</u> and should take about <u>10 minutes</u> to complete.

- Each test starts with some <u>warm-up questions</u> to get you going and ends with a <u>problem-solving question</u>.

- The tests <u>increase in difficulty</u> as you go through the book.

- <u>Answers</u> and a <u>Progress Chart</u> can be found at the <u>back</u> of the book.

Test 1

Warm up

1. Circle the pair of lily pads that have a total of 10 frogs.

    _____
    1 mark

2. Write a number so that each pair adds up to 20.

    a) 7 and ....   b) 12 and ....

    _____
    1 mark

3. Fill in the boxes with + or − to make the number sentences correct.

    6 ☐ 3 = 9   9 ☐ 2 = 7

    8 ☐ 7 = 1   4 ☐ 2 = 6

    _____
    2 marks

4. Draw lines to match the sums with their answers.

12 add 6   17

17 subtract 0   7

3 add 13   18

19 subtract 12   16

2 marks

5. Ali has two dark pencils and three light pencils.

How many pencils does Ali have in total?

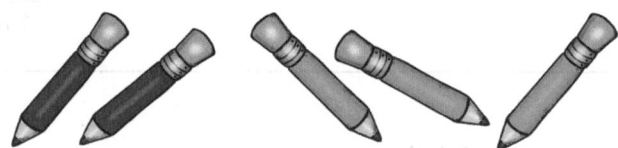

....

1 mark

6. Jofra has seven pets.
Three are cats and the rest are guinea pigs.

Write this as a sum.

3 + ... = ...

1 mark

END OF TEST

/ 8

Test 2

Warm up

1. Circle the sums that add up to twenty.

    15 add 5   9 add 9

    14 add 8   13 add 7

    1 mark

2. Jules subtracts 2 from 14 to get 12.

    Circle the sum she did.

    2 + 12 = 14   14 − 2 = 12   14 − 12 = 2

    1 mark

3. Put an equals sign and an addition sign in this sum to make it correct.

    1 ☐ 12 ☐ 13

    1 mark

    Put an equals sign and a subtraction sign in this sum to make it correct.

    13 ☐ 12 ☐ 1

    1 mark

4. Fill in the missing numbers.

   5 + 14 = ...

   .... + 4 = 12

   2 marks

5. Lucy is thinking of a number.
   It is five more than twelve.

   What number is Lucy thinking of?

   ....
   1 mark

6. Levi adds a number to itself to get twelve.

   What is his number?

   ....
   1 mark

   END OF TEST

   / 8

Test 3

Warm up

1. Write the number that is...

   a) ... five less than fifteen   ....

   b) ... nine less than twenty   ....

   2 marks

2. Complete the matching subtraction for each addition.

   12 + 4 = 16   16 – 4 = ...

   15 + 3 = 18   .... – 3 = ...

   2 marks

3. Work out the answers to these subtractions.

   19 – 13 = ...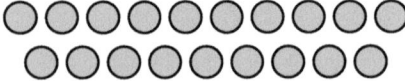

   17 – 5 = ...

   1 mark

4. Use the number line to fill in the missing numbers.

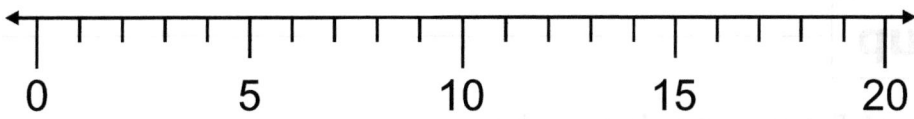

19 − .... = 11

17 − .... = 3

1 mark

5. Lisa gives 6 chocolate cookies to Felix and 13 chocolate cookies to Maria.

How many cookies does she give away in total?

....
1 mark

Felix already had 7 raisin cookies.

How many cookies does Felix have in total now?

....
1 mark

END OF TEST

/ 8

Test 4

Warm up

1. Subtract 5 from each number.

   a) 20 ....   b) 13 ....

   1 mark

2. Circle the sum that gives the biggest answer.

   17 – 3   13 + 4   12 + 2

   1 mark

3. Match each sum with its missing number.

   12 + 3 = ☐   7

   11 + ☐ = 18   17

   8 + 9 = ☐   9

   7 + ☐ = 16   15

   2 marks

4. Write the answers to each sum.

 0 + 10 = ...   10 − 0 = ...

 15 + 9 = ...   16 − 8 = ...

 2 marks

5. Josie is thinking of a number.
   She says "It's fourteen less than eighteen."

   What number is she thinking of?

   .... 1 mark

6. Otis is thinking of the number eleven.

   Fill in the missing word in his sentence.

   "It's .... less than nineteen."   1 mark

END OF TEST

/ 8

Test 5

Warm up

1. Join the pairs of numbers that add up to 15.

6   7

5   8

4   9

11 10

2 marks

2. Use the number line to fill in the missing number.

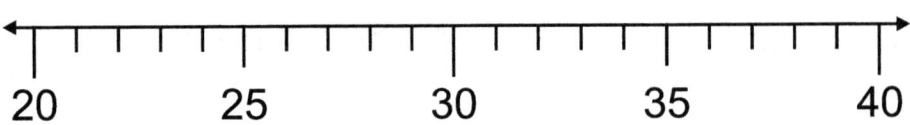

27 + ... = 30

1 mark

3. Fill in the missing numbers below.

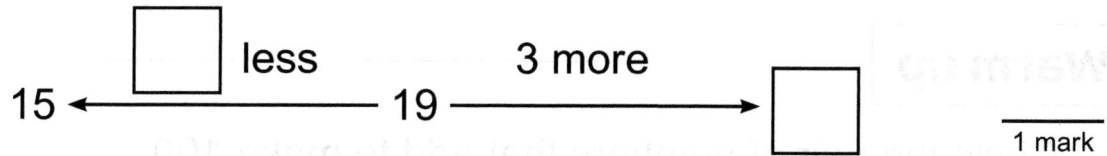

 ___
 1 mark

4. Write the answers to these sums.

 22 + 3 = ...

 22 + 30 = ...

 ___
 2 marks

5. 32 can be broken up into 3 tens and 2 ones.

 Use this to work out 27 + 32.

 ....
 ___
 2 marks

END OF TEST

/ 8

Test 6

Warm up

1. Circle the pair of numbers that add to make 100.

   30   50   80   70   40

   1 mark

2. What is:

   a) one more than forty-two?   ....

   b) one less than forty-two?   ....

   1 mark

3. Draw lines to match the sums with their answers.

   | 29 − 7 | | 1 |

   | 32 − 20 | | 12 |

   | 23 − 22 | | 22 |

   2 marks

4. A squirrel has 23 acorns. He collects 6 more.

   How many acorns does he have now?

   23 + ... = ...

   1 mark

5. Complete the sums using numbers from the box.

   You can use numbers more than once.

   | 39 | 34 | 5 |

   34 + ... = ...

   .... − 34 = ...

   1 mark

6. Doug collects conkers. He smashes 2 and collects 4 more. He now has 33 conkers.

   How many conkers did Doug start with?

   ....

   2 marks

   END OF TEST

   / 8

Test 7

Warm up

1. Work out these sums.

   a) 21 + 5 = ...

   b) 32 + 7 = ...

   1 mark

2. Janelle has 35 sea shells.
   She sells 12 at a car boot sale.

   How many sea shells does she have now?

   ....

   1 mark

3. Fill in the missing word in this sentence.

   I'm thinking of a number.

   It's 5 less than 36 and 3 more than ....

   2 marks

4. Harry knows that if 1 and 1 make 2,
then 10 and 10 make 20.

Complete the rest of Harry's sentences.

"If 4 and 6 make 10,

then .... and .... make 100."

"If 9 and 1 make 10,

then .... and 10 make ...."

2 marks

5. Use the grey number cards to complete the two different sums. Use the cards as many times as you like.

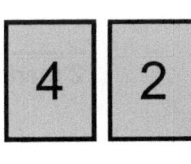

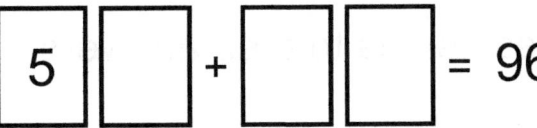

2 marks

END OF TEST

/ 8

Test 8

Warm up

1. Geraldine starts with the number 10.
   She adds 5, then subtracts 5.

   What number is she left with?

   ....
   1 mark

2. Write down a correct addition, and a subtraction you could do to check it. Only use numbers in the box.

   | 60   17   77 |

   60 + ☐ = ☐

   ☐ − ☐ = ☐

   2 marks

3. Match these sums to their answers.

   | 36 − 25 | | 49 − 37 | | 39 − 19 |

   | 11 | | 20 | | 12 |

   2 marks

4. Circle the sums that are correct.

29 + 45 = 45 + 29

37 − 15 = 15 − 37

18 + 5 − 5 = 18

1 mark

5. Maxine is saving to buy a new hover board for £87.

Her grandma gives her £24.

Her dad gives her £18.

Fill in the gaps to work out how much more money she needs.

£18 + £24 = £..................

1 mark

£87 − £.................. = £..................

1 mark

END OF TEST

/ 8

Test 9

Warm up

1. Circle the sums that give the same answer as 8 + 7 + 9.

   7 + 8 + 9   7 + 9 + 8

   9 − 7 − 8   8 + 9 + 7

   _____
   1 mark

2. Fill in the missing number.

   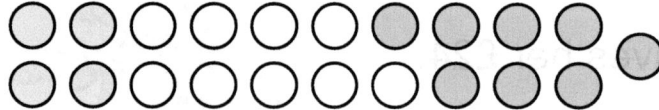

   4 + ... + 8 = 21

   _____
   1 mark

3. There are 37 toys in a shop.

   The shop sells 17 and buys 29 more.

   How many toys are there in the shop now?

   ....   _____
   2 marks

Test 9

4. Myra and Tom are playing snakes and ladders. Myra is on square 27. She rolls this number on a dice and moves forward.

What square does she land on?

.... 1 mark

Tom is on square 41. He rolls the dice below and moves that number of squares forward. He lands on a ladder that takes him 9 more squares forward.

 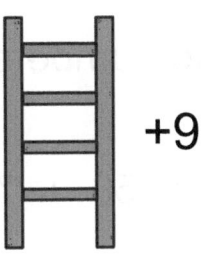 +9

What square is he on now?

.... 2 marks

On Myra's last turn she lands on square 65 and slides back 57 squares on a snake.

What square does she finish on?

.... 1 mark

END OF TEST

/ 8

Test 10

Warm up

1. Answer these sums:

   a) 37 + 8 − 8 = ...   b) 3 + 7 + 3 = ...

   c) 45 + 15 = ...   d) 15 + 45 = ...

   2 marks

2. Fill in the missing numbers in these sums.

   79 + 45 + 56 = 56 + 79 + ...

   32 + 48 + ... = 48 + 61 + 32

   2 marks

3. Ryan chooses a raffle ticket number by adding up the ages of himself and his two brothers.

   Ryan is 9   Jack is 6   Dean is 5

   What is his raffle ticket number?

   ....

   1 mark

4. Fill in the gaps to show how to check the answer to this sum.

$$43 - 25 = 18$$

.... + ... = ...

1 mark

5. Leena is playing a game.
She picks two cards and has to pick one more.

What is the total of these two cards?

....
1 mark

Circle the card she should pick to give a total of 51.

1 mark

END OF TEST

/ 8

Test 11

Warm up

1. Work out these sums.

    a) 40 + 30 + 10 = ...

    b) 70 + 20 + 20 = ...

    1 mark

2. Write four different correct sums using these numbers.

    | 4 | 27 | 31 |

    .... + ... = ...

    .... + ... = ...

    .... − .... = ...

    .... − .... = ...

    2 marks

3. Jameelia runs 92 m.
   This is 17 m further than Naomi.

   How far does Naomi run?

   .... m   1 mark

4. Fill in the missing numbers in these sums.

   79 – .... = 60   .... – 23 = 40

   2 marks

5. Maggie had 84 g of sugar.
   She spilled some. She only has 56 g now.
   How much did she spill?

   .... g   1 mark

   She needs 75 g for her recipe.
   How much more does she need after the spill?

   .... g   1 mark

   END OF TEST   / 8

Test 12

Warm up

1. Circle the two piles of money that add up to £70.

£55   £25   £45

£40   £65   £20

1 mark

2. There's £6 in a charity money box.

   Richard adds £3 and Jo adds £7.

   How much money is in the box now?

   £ ....

   1 mark

3. Fill in the missing number in these sums.

   42 + ... = 67   .... + 31 = 63

   2 marks

4. Work out these sums.

   45 + 35 = ...

   37 + 52 = ...

   2 marks

5. Jackson has collected 35 trading cards.

   There are 98 to collect.

   How many cards does he have left to collect?

   .... 1 mark

   Ayubu has collected 47 cards.

   How many more cards has he collected than Jackson?

   .... 1 mark

   END OF TEST

   / 8

Answers

Test 1 – pages 2-3

1. These two pictures should be circled

   (**1 mark for both correct**)

2. a) 7 and 13
   b) 12 and 8
   (**1 mark for both correct**)

3. 6 + 3 = 9   9 – 2 = 7
   8 – 7 = 1   4 + 2 = 6
   (**2 marks for all four correct, otherwise 1 mark for two correct**)

4.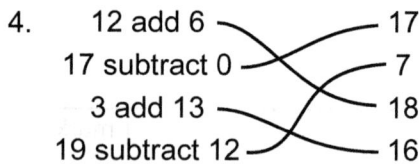

   (**2 marks for all four lines correct, otherwise 1 mark for two lines correct**)

5. 2 + 3 = 5
   So Ali has 5 pencils. (**1 mark**)

6. 3 + 4 = 7 (**1 mark**)

Test 2 – pages 4-5

1. 15 add 5 and 13 add 7 should be circled. (**1 mark for both correct**)
2. 14 – 2 = 12 should be circled. (**1 mark**)
3. 1 + 12 = 13 (**1 mark**)
   13 – 12 = 1 (**1 mark**)
4. 5 + 14 = 19 (**1 mark**)
   8 + 4 = 12 (**1 mark**)
5. 12 + 5 = 17, so Lucy is thinking of 17. (**1 mark**)
6. 6 + 6 = 12, so Levi adds 6 to itself. (**1 mark**)

Test 3 – pages 6-7

1. a) 10 (**1 mark**)
   b) 11 (**1 mark**)
2. 16 – 4 = 12 (**1 mark**)
   18 – 3 = 15 (**1 mark**)
3. 19 – 13 = 6   17 – 5 = 12
   (**1 mark for both correct**)
4. 19 – 8 = 11
   17 – 14 = 3
   (**1 mark for both correct**)
5. 13 + 6 = 19
   So Lisa gives away 19 cookies.
   (**1 mark**)
   7 + 6 = 13
   So Felix has 13 cookies.
   (**1 mark**)

Test 4 – pages 8-9

1. a) 15   b) 8
   (**1 mark for both correct**)
2. 13 + 4 should be circled (**1 mark**)
3.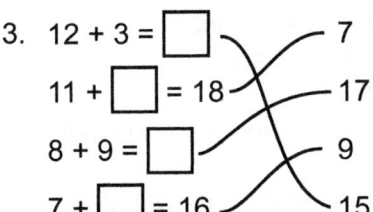

   (**2 marks for all four lines correct, otherwise 1 mark for two lines correct**)
4. 0 + 10 = 10   10 − 0 = 10
   15 + 9 = 24   16 − 8 = 8
   (**2 marks for all four correct, otherwise 1 mark for two correct**)
5. Josie is thinking of 4. (**1 mark**)
6. Otis's missing word is eight. (**1 mark**)

Test 5 – pages 10-11

1.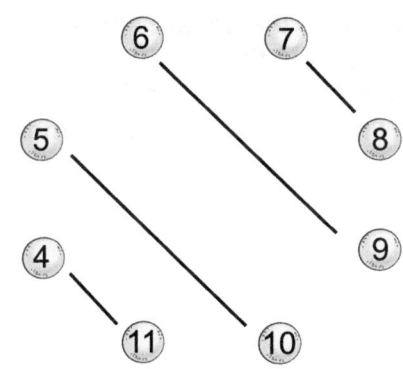

   (**2 marks for all four lines correct, otherwise 1 mark for two lines correct**)
2. 27 + 3 = 30 (**1 mark**)
3. 15 ←(4 less)— 19 —(3 more)→ 22
   (**1 mark for both correct**)

4. 25 (**1 mark**)
   52 (**1 mark**)
5. 27 plus 3 tens is 57
   57 plus 2 ones is 59
   So 27 + 32 = 59
   (**2 marks for the correct answer, otherwise 1 mark for a correct method**)

Test 6 – pages 12-13

1. 30 and 70 should be circled (**1 mark**)
2. a) 43
   b) 41
   (**1 mark for both correct**)
3.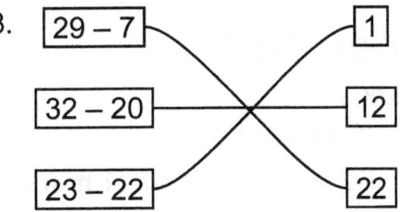

   (**2 marks for all three lines correct, otherwise 1 mark for two lines correct**)
4. 23 + 6 = 29 (**1 mark**)
5. 34 + 5 = 39
   39 − 34 = 5
   (**1 mark for all four correct**)
6. He has 33, so subtract the 4 he collected to find how many he had before: 33 − 4 = 29
   Then add the 2 that he smashed to see how many he had to start with: 29 + 2 = 31
   So Doug started with 31 conkers.
   (**2 marks for the correct answer, otherwise 1 mark for a correct method**)

Test 7 – pages 14-15

1. a) 26 b) 39
   (**1 mark for both correct**)
2. 35 − 12 = 23 (**1 mark**)
3. 5 less than 36 is 31, and 31 is 3 more than 28, so the answer is 28.
   (**2 marks for the correct answer, otherwise 1 mark for working out 31**)
4. If 4 and 6 make 10, then 40 and 60 make 100. (**1 mark**)
   If 9 and 1 make 10, then 90 and 10 make 100. (**1 mark**)
5. 52 + 24 = 76 or 54 + 22 = 76 (**1 mark**)
   54 + 42 = 96 or 52 + 44 = 96 (**1 mark**)

Test 8 – pages 16-17

1. 10 (**1 mark**)
2. 60 + 17 = 77 (**1 mark**)
   77 − 17 = 60 or 77 − 60 = 17 (**1 mark**)
3.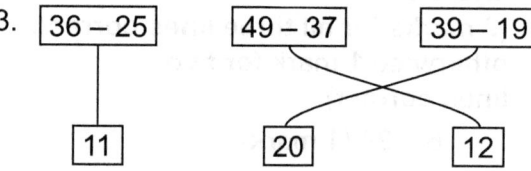

   (**2 marks for all three lines correct, otherwise 1 mark for 2 lines correct**)
4. 29 + 45 = 45 + 29 and 18 + 5 − 5 = 18 should be circled. (**1 mark**)
5. Partition £24 into £20 and £4.
   £18 + £20 = £38 and £38 + £4 = £42, so the first calculation is:
   £18 + £24 = £42 (**1 mark**)
   £87 − £42 = £45 (**1 mark**)

Test 9 – pages 18-19

1. 7 + 8 + 9, 7 + 9 + 8 and 8 + 9 + 7 should be circled. (**1 mark**)
2. 4 + 9 + 8 = 21 (**1 mark**)
3. Starting with 37, subtract the number of toys sold:
   37 − 17 = 20
   Then add the number of toys bought:
   20 + 29 = 49
   So there are 49 toys in the shop.
   (**2 marks for the correct answer, otherwise 1 mark for a correct method**)
4. Add the dice roll of 6 to the square Myra was on:
   27 + 6 = 33 (**1 mark**)
   Add the dice roll to the square Tom was on:
   41 + 5 = 46
   Then add the extra 9 squares from going up the ladder:
   46 + 9 = 55
   (**2 marks for the correct answer, otherwise 1 mark for working out 46**)
   Subtract the number of squares Myra slid back from the square she was on. Partition 57 into 50 and 7.
   65 − 50 = 15 and 15 − 7 = 8, so she finishes on square 8. (**1 mark**)

Answers

Test 10 – pages 20-21

1. a) 37   b) 13   c) 60   d) 60
   (**2 marks for all three correct, otherwise 1 mark for two correct**)
2. 79 + 45 + 56 = 56 + 79 + 45 (**1 mark**)
   32 + 48 + 61 = 48 + 61 + 32 (**1 mark**)
3. 9 + 6 + 5 = 15 + 5 = 20, so his raffle ticket number is 20. (**1 mark**)
4. 18 + 25 = 43 or 25 + 18 = 43 (**1 mark**)
5. Add up the numbers on the two cards.
   Partition 17 into 10 and 7.
   26 + 10 = 36 and 36 + 7 = 43,
   so the total is 43. (**1 mark**)

   Subtract the total of the two cards she has already picked from 51.
   Partition 43 into 40 and 3. 51 – 40 = 11 and 11 – 3 = 8, so 51 – 43 = 8.
   So 8 should be circled. (**1 mark**)

Test 11 – pages 22-23

1. a) 80   b) 110
   (**1 mark for both correct**)
2. 4 + 27 = 31
   27 + 4 = 31
   31 – 4 = 27
   31 – 27 = 4
   (**2 marks for all four correct, otherwise 1 mark for at least two correct**)
3. Subtract 17 m from the distance Jameelia runs. Partition 17 into 10 and 7. 92 m – 10 m = 82 m and 82 m – 7 m = 75 m.
   So Naomi runs 75 m. (**1 mark**)
4. 79 – 19 = 60 (**1 mark**)
   63 – 23 = 40 (**1 mark**)
5. Subtract the amount she has left from the amount she started with.
   Partition 56 into 50 and 6.
   84 g – 50 g = 34 g and
   34 g – 6 g = 28 g,
   so 84 g – 56 g = 28 g.
   So she spilt 28 g. (**1 mark**)

   Subtract the amount she has left from the amount she needs:
   75 g – 50 g = 25 g and
   25 g – 6 g = 19 g,
   so 75 g – 56 g = 19 g.
   So she needs 19 g more. (**1 mark**)

Test 12 – pages 24-25

1. The £25 and £45 piles should be circled. (**1 mark**)
2. There is £6 + £3 + £7 = £9 + £7 = £16 in the box now. (**1 mark**)
3. 42 + 25 = 67 (**1 mark**)
   32 + 31 = 63 (**1 mark**)
4. 45 + 35 = 80 (**1 mark**)
   37 + 52 = 89 (**1 mark**)
5. Subtract the number of cards he has already collected:
   98 – 35 = 63
   So he has 63 cards left to collect.
   (**1 mark**)

   Subtract the number of cards Jackson has collected from the number of cards Ayubu has collected:
   47 – 35 = 12
   So he has 12 more cards. (**1 mark**)

Progress Chart

That's all the tests in the book done — nice one!

Now fill in this table with all of your scores and see how you got on.

	Score
Test 1	
Test 2	
Test 3	
Test 4	
Test 5	
Test 6	
Test 7	
Test 8	
Test 9	
Test 10	
Test 11	
Test 12	